This Book
BELONGS TO

← ─────────────────────────────── →

← ─────────────────────────────── →

← ─────────────────────────────── →

← ─────────────────────────────── →

← ─────────────────────────────── →

← ─────────────────────────────── →

Date:	Let's do this!	M T W T F S S

My 3 top priorities for today

1		☐
2		☐
3		☐

To do list	Water	Appointments

To do list		Water	Appointments
	☐	1	
	☐	☐ 2	
	☐	☐ 3	
	☐	☐ 4	

Schedule AM	☐ 5	Schedule PM
	☐ 6	
	☐ 7	
	☐ 8	
	☐	

Food

B	D
L	S

Health & Fitness	I am thankful for...

Date: _____   **Let's do this!**   M T W T F S S

My 3 top priorities for today

1 _____ ☐

2 _____ ☐

3 _____ ☐

To do list	Water	Appointments

☐	1 ☐	
☐	2 ☐	
☐	3 ☐	
☐	4 ☐	

Schedule AM		Schedule PM
	5 ☐	
	6 ☐	
	7 ☐	
	8 ☐	

Food

B	D
L	S

Health & Fitness	I am thankful for...

Date: _____   Let's do this!   M T W T F S S

My 3 top priorities for today

1 _____ ☐

2 _____ ☐

3 _____ ☐

To do list	Water	Appointments

To do list		Water	Appointments
☐	1 ☐	
☐	2 ☐	
☐	3 ☐	
☐	4 ☐	

Schedule AM	Water	Schedule PM
	5 ☐	
	6 ☐	
	7 ☐	
	8 ☐	

Food

B	D
L	S

Health & Fitness	I am thankful for...

Date:	Let's do this!	M T W T F S S

My 3 top priorities for today

1 ☐

2 ☐

3 ☐

To do list	Water	Appointments

	☐	1 ☐	
	☐	2 ☐	
	☐	3 ☐	
	☐	4 ☐	

Schedule AM	5 ☐	Schedule PM
	6 ☐	
	7 ☐	
	8 ☐	
	☐	

Food

B	D
L	S

Health & Fitness	I am thankful for...

Date: _____   ## Let's do this!   M T W T F S S

My 3 top priorities for today

1 _____ ☐

2 _____ ☐

3 _____ ☐

To do list	Water	Appointments
☐	1	
☐	☐ 2	
☐	☐ 3	
☐	☐ 4	

Schedule AM	☐ 5	Schedule PM
	☐ 6	
	☐ 7	
	☐ 8	
	☐	

Food

B	D
L	S

Health & Fitness	I am thankful for...

Date: _____   **Let's do this!**   M T W T F S S

My 3 top priorities for today

1 _____ ☐

2 _____ ☐

3 _____ ☐

To do list	Water	Appointments

To do list		Water	Appointments
_____ ☐	1 ☐	
_____ ☐	2 ☐	
_____ ☐	3 ☐	
_____ ☐	4 ☐	

Schedule AM		Water	Schedule PM
	5 ☐	
	6 ☐	
	7 ☐	
	8 ☐	

Food

B	D
L	S

Health & Fitness	I am thankful for...

Date: **Let's do this!** M T W T F S S

My 3 top priorities for today

1 ☐

2 ☐

3 ☐

To do list	Water	Appointments

To do list:
- ☐
- ☐
- ☐
- ☐

Water:
1 ☐
2 ☐
3 ☐
4 ☐
5 ☐
6 ☐
7 ☐
8 ☐

Schedule AM

Schedule PM

Food

B

D

L

S

Health & Fitness	I am thankful for...

Date: _____ **Let's do this!** M T W T F S S

My 3 top priorities for today

1 _____ ☐

2 _____ ☐

3 _____ ☐

To do list	Water	Appointments

To do list		Water	Appointments
_____ ☐	1 ☐	_____
_____ ☐	2 ☐	_____
_____ ☐	3 ☐	_____
_____ ☐	4 ☐	_____

Schedule AM		Schedule PM
	5 ☐	
	6 ☐	
	7 ☐	
	8 ☐	

Food

B	D
L	S

Health & Fitness	I am thankful for...

Date:	Let's do this!	M T W T F S S

My 3 top priorities for today

1 ☐

2 ☐

3 ☐

To do list	Water	Appointments

To do list		Water	Appointments
	☐	1	
	☐	☐ 2	
	☐	☐ 3	
	☐	☐ 4	

Schedule AM		Schedule PM
	☐ 5	
	☐ 6	
	☐ 7	
	☐ 8	
	☐	

Food

B	D
L	S

Health & Fitness	I am thankful for...

Date: _____ Let's do this! M T W T F S S

My 3 top priorities for today

1 ☐

2 ☐

3 ☐

To do list	Water	Appointments
☐	1	
☐	☐ 2	
☐	☐ 3	
☐	☐ 4	

Schedule AM	☐ 5	Schedule PM
	☐ 6	
	☐ 7	
	☐ 8	
	☐	

Food

B	D
L	S

Health & Fitness	I am thankful for...

Date: Let's do this!   M T W T F S S

My 3 top priorities for today

1   ☐

2   ☐

3   ☐

To do list	Water	Appointments
☐	1 ☐	
☐	2 ☐	
☐	3 ☐	
☐	4 ☐	

Schedule AM	5 ☐	Schedule PM
	6 ☐	
	7 ☐	
	8 ☐	
	☐	

Food

B | D

L | S

Health & Fitness	I am thankful for...

Date: _____ Let's do this! M T W T F S S

My 3 top priorities for today

1 ☐

2 ☐

3 ☐

To do list	Water	Appointments

To do list:
- ☐
- ☐
- ☐
- ☐

Water:
1 ☐
2 ☐
3 ☐
4 ☐
5 ☐
6 ☐
7 ☐
8 ☐

Schedule AM

Schedule PM

Food

B

D

L

S

Health & Fitness

I am thankful for...

Date: _____ **Let's do this!**   M T W T F S S

My 3 top priorities for today

1 _____ ☐

2 _____ ☐

3 _____ ☐

To do list	Water	Appointments

To do list
- ☐
- ☐
- ☐
- ☐

Water
1 ☐
2 ☐
3 ☐
4 ☐
5 ☐
6 ☐
7 ☐
8 ☐

Schedule AM

Schedule PM

Food

B

D

L

S

Health & Fitness	I am thankful for...

Date:	Let's do this!	M T W T F S S

My 3 top priorities for today

1 ☐

2 ☐

3 ☐

To do list	Water	Appointments

		☐	1 ☐	
		☐	2 ☐	
		☐	3 ☐	
		☐	4 ☐	

Schedule AM	5 ☐	Schedule PM
	6 ☐	
	7 ☐	
	8 ☐	

Food

B	D
L	S

Health & Fitness	I am thankful for...

Date: _____   **Let's do this!**   M T W T F S S

My 3 top priorities for today

1 _____ ☐

2 _____ ☐

3 _____ ☐

To do list	Water	Appointments

To do list:
☐
☐
☐
☐

Water:
1 ☐
2 ☐
3 ☐
4 ☐
5 ☐
6 ☐
7 ☐
8 ☐

Schedule AM

Schedule PM

Food

B _____ | D _____

L _____ | S _____

Health & Fitness	I am thankful for...

Date: **Let's do this!** M T W T F S S

My 3 top priorities for today

1 ☐

2 ☐

3 ☐

To do list	Water	Appointments

To do list:
- ☐
- ☐
- ☐
- ☐

Water:
1 ☐
2 ☐
3 ☐
4 ☐
5 ☐
6 ☐
7 ☐
8 ☐

Schedule AM

Schedule PM

Food

B

D

L

S

Health & Fitness	I am thankful for...

Date:	Let's do this!	M T W T F S S

My 3 top priorities for today

1	☐
2	☐
3	☐

To do list	Water	Appointments

	☐	1 ☐	
	☐	2 ☐	
	☐	3 ☐	
	☐	4 ☐	

Schedule AM		Schedule PM
	5 ☐	
	6 ☐	
	7 ☐	
	8 ☐	

Food

B	D
L	S

Health & Fitness	I am thankful for...

Date:	Let's do this!	M T W T F S S

My 3 top priorities for today

1. ☐
2. ☐
3. ☐

To do list	Water	Appointments

To do list		Water	Appointments
	☐	1 ☐	
	☐	2 ☐	
	☐	3 ☐	
	☐	4 ☐	

Schedule AM	Water	Schedule PM
	5 ☐	
	6 ☐	
	7 ☐	
	8 ☐	

Food

B	D
L	S

Health & Fitness	I am thankful for...

Date: # Let's do this!   M T W T F S S

My 3 top priorities for today

1   ☐

2   ☐

3   ☐

To do list	Water	Appointments
☐	1 ☐	
☐	2 ☐	
☐	3 ☐	
☐	4 ☐	

Schedule AM		Schedule PM
	5 ☐	
	6 ☐	
	7 ☐	
	8 ☐	

Food

B	D
L	S

Health & Fitness	I am thankful for...

Date:	Let's do this!	M T W T F S S

My 3 top priorities for today

1 ☐

2 ☐

3 ☐

To do list	Water	Appointments

☐

☐

☐

☐

1 ☐
2 ☐
3 ☐
4 ☐
5 ☐
6 ☐
7 ☐
8 ☐

Schedule AM		Schedule PM

Food

B

D

L

S

Health & Fitness	I am thankful for...

Date: Let's do this!   M T W T F S S

My 3 top priorities for today

1 ☐

2 ☐

3 ☐

To do list	Water	Appointments

☐

☐ 1
☐
☐ 2
☐
☐ 3
☐
☐ 4

Schedule AM	5	Schedule PM

☐ 6

☐ 7

☐ 8

☐

Food

B | D

L | S

Health & Fitness	I am thankful for...

Date: _____   # Let's do this!   M T W T F S S

My 3 top priorities for today

1. _____ ☐
2. _____ ☐
3. _____ ☐

To do list	Water	Appointments

To do list
- ☐
- ☐
- ☐
- ☐

Water
1 ☐
2 ☐
3 ☐
4 ☐
5 ☐
6 ☐
7 ☐
8 ☐

Schedule AM

Schedule PM

Food

B

D

L

S

Health & Fitness

I am thankful for...

Date:	Let's do this!	M T W T F S S

My 3 top priorities for today

1. ☐
2. ☐
3. ☐

To do list	Water	Appointments

☐
☐
☐
☐

1 ☐
2 ☐
3 ☐
4 ☐
5 ☐
6 ☐
7 ☐
8 ☐

Schedule AM

Schedule PM

Food

B

D

L

S

Health & Fitness

I am thankful for...

Date: _____ Let's do this! M T W T F S S

My 3 top priorities for today

1. ☐
2. ☐
3. ☐

To do list	Water	Appointments

To do list
- ☐
- ☐
- ☐
- ☐

Water
1 ☐
2 ☐
3 ☐
4 ☐
5 ☐
6 ☐
7 ☐
8 ☐

Schedule AM

Schedule PM

Food

B

D

L

S

Health & Fitness	I am thankful for...

Date: **Let's do this!**   M T W T F S S

My 3 top priorities for today

1   ☐

2   ☐

3   ☐

To do list	Water	Appointments
☐	1 ☐	
☐	2 ☐	
☐	3 ☐	
☐	4 ☐	

Schedule AM		Schedule PM
	5 ☐	
	6 ☐	
	7 ☐	
	8 ☐	

Food

B	D
L	S

Health & Fitness	I am thankful for...

Date: **Let's do this!**   M T W T F S S

My 3 top priorities for today

1   ☐

2   ☐

3   ☐

To do list	Water	Appointments
☐	1 ☐	
☐	2 ☐	
☐	3 ☐	
☐	4 ☐	

Schedule AM	Water	Schedule PM
	5 ☐	
	6 ☐	
	7 ☐	
	8 ☐	

Food

B	D
L	S

Health & Fitness	I am thankful for...

Date:	Let's do this!	M T W T F S S

My 3 top priorities for today

1. ☐
2. ☐
3. ☐

To do list	Water	Appointments
☐	1 ☐	
☐	2 ☐	
☐	3 ☐	
☐	4 ☐	

Schedule AM		Schedule PM
	5 ☐	
	6 ☐	
	7 ☐	
	8 ☐	

Food

B	D
L	S

Health & Fitness	I am thankful for...

Date:	Let's do this!	M T W T F S S

My 3 top priorities for today

1	☐
2	☐
3	☐

To do list	Water	Appointments

To do list		Water	Appointments
☐	1 ☐	
☐	2 ☐	
☐	3 ☐	
☐	4 ☐	

Schedule AM	Water	Schedule PM

Schedule AM		Water	Schedule PM
	5 ☐	
	6 ☐	
	7 ☐	
	8 ☐	

Food

B	D
L	S

Health & Fitness	I am thankful for...

Let's do this!

Date: _____   M T W T F S S

My 3 top priorities for today

1 _____ ☐

2 _____ ☐

3 _____ ☐

To do list	Water	Appointments
☐	1 ☐	
☐	2 ☐	
☐	3 ☐	
☐	4 ☐	

Schedule AM		Schedule PM
	5 ☐	
	6 ☐	
	7 ☐	
	8 ☐	

Food

B _____ | D _____

L _____ | S _____

Health & Fitness	I am thankful for...

Date: **Let's do this!** M T W T F S S

My 3 top priorities for today

1. ☐
2. ☐
3. ☐

To do list	Water	Appointments
☐	1	
☐	☐ 2	
☐	☐ 3	
☐	☐ 4	

Schedule AM	☐ 5	Schedule PM
	☐ 6	
	☐ 7	
	☐ 8	
	☐	

Food

B	D
L	S

Health & Fitness	I am thankful for...

Date: Let's do this!   M T W T F S S

My 3 top priorities for today

1   ☐

2   ☐

3   ☐

To do list	Water	Appointments
☐	1 ☐	
☐	2 ☐	
☐	3 ☐	
☐	4 ☐	

Schedule AM	Water	Schedule PM
	5 ☐	
	6 ☐	
	7 ☐	
	8 ☐	
	☐	

Food

B	D
L	S

Health & Fitness	I am thankful for...

Date: _____   *Let's do this!*   M T W T F S S

My 3 top priorities for today

1	☐
2	☐
3	☐

To do list	Water	Appointments

To do list
- ☐
- ☐
- ☐
- ☐

Water
1 ☐
2 ☐
3 ☐
4 ☐
5 ☐
6 ☐
7 ☐
8 ☐

Schedule AM		Schedule PM

Food

B	D
L	S

Health & Fitness	I am thankful for...

Date: # Let's do this!   M T W T F S S

My 3 top priorities for today

1   ☐

2   ☐

3   ☐

To do list	Water	Appointments
☐	1 ☐	
☐	2 ☐	
☐	3 ☐	
☐	4 ☐	

Schedule AM		Schedule PM
	5 ☐	
	6 ☐	
	7 ☐	
	8 ☐	

Food

B	D
L	S

Health & Fitness	I am thankful for...

Date: _____ **Let's do this!** M T W T F S S

My 3 top priorities for today

1	☐
2	☐
3	☐

To do list	Water	Appointments

To do list		Water	Appointments
	☐	1 ☐	
	☐	2 ☐	
	☐	3 ☐	
	☐	4 ☐	
Schedule AM		5 ☐	**Schedule PM**
		6 ☐	
		7 ☐	
		8 ☐	

Food

B	D
L	S

Health & Fitness	I am thankful for...

Date: # Let's do this!   M T W T F S S

My 3 top priorities for today

1 ☐

2 ☐

3 ☐

To do list	Water	Appointments

- ☐
- ☐
- ☐
- ☐

1 ☐
2 ☐
3 ☐
4 ☐
5 ☐
6 ☐
7 ☐
8 ☐

Schedule AM   Schedule PM

Food

B

D

L

S

Health & Fitness   I am thankful for...

Date: Let's do this!   M T W T F S S

My 3 top priorities for today

1 ☐

2 ☐

3 ☐

To do list	Water	Appointments
☐		
☐	1 ☐	
☐	2 ☐	
☐	3 ☐	

Schedule AM	4 ☐	Schedule PM
	5 ☐	
	6 ☐	
	7 ☐	
	8 ☐	

Food

B	D
L	S

Health & Fitness	I am thankful for...

Date:	Let's do this!	M T W T F S S

My 3 top priorities for today

1. ☐
2. ☐
3. ☐

To do list	Water	Appointments

To do list
- ☐
- ☐
- ☐
- ☐

Water
1 ☐
2 ☐
3 ☐
4 ☐
5 ☐
6 ☐
7 ☐
8 ☐

Schedule AM		Schedule PM

Food

B	D
L	S

Health & Fitness	I am thankful for...

Date: _____ Let's do this! M T W T F S S

My 3 top priorities for today

1 ☐

2 ☐

3 ☐

To do list	Water	Appointments
☐	1 ☐	
☐	2 ☐	
☐	3 ☐	
☐	4 ☐	
Schedule AM	5 ☐	**Schedule PM**
	6 ☐	
	7 ☐	
	8 ☐	

Food

B	D
L	S

Health & Fitness	I am thankful for...

Date: *Let's do this!*   M T W T F S S

My 3 top priorities for today

1   ☐

2   ☐

3   ☐

To do list	Water	Appointments
☐	1 ☐	
☐	2 ☐	
☐	3 ☐	
☐	4 ☐	

Schedule AM		Schedule PM
	5 ☐	
	6 ☐	
	7 ☐	
	8 ☐	

Food

B	D
L	S

Health & Fitness	I am thankful for...

Date: Let's do this!   M T W T F S S

My 3 top priorities for today

1 ☐

2 ☐

3 ☐

To do list	Water	Appointments

☐

☐

☐

☐

1 ☐
2 ☐
3 ☐
4 ☐
5 ☐
6 ☐
7 ☐
8 ☐

Schedule AM

Schedule PM

Food

B

D

L

S

Health & Fitness	I am thankful for...

Date: _____ # Let's do this! M T W T F S S

My 3 top priorities for today

1. ☐
2. ☐
3. ☐

To do list	Water	Appointments

To do list
- ☐
- ☐
- ☐
- ☐

Water
1 ☐
2 ☐
3 ☐
4 ☐
5 ☐
6 ☐
7 ☐
8 ☐

Schedule AM

Schedule PM

Food

B:

D:

L:

S:

Health & Fitness

I am thankful for...

Date: _____   **Let's do this!**   M T W T F S S

My 3 top priorities for today

1 _____ ☐

2 _____ ☐

3 _____ ☐

To do list	Water	Appointments

☐	1 ☐	
☐	2 ☐	
☐	3 ☐	
☐	4 ☐	

Schedule AM	5 ☐	Schedule PM
	6 ☐	
	7 ☐	
	8 ☐	
	☐	

Food

B	D
L	S

Health & Fitness	I am thankful for...

Date: Let's do this!   M T W T F S S

My 3 top priorities for today

1   ☐

2   ☐

3   ☐

To do list	Water	Appointments
☐	1 ☐	
☐	2 ☐	
☐	3 ☐	
☐	4 ☐	

Schedule AM		Schedule PM
	5 ☐	
	6 ☐	
	7 ☐	
	8 ☐	
	☐	

Food

B   D

L   S

Health & Fitness	I am thankful for...

Date: _____ Let's do this!   M T W T F S S

My 3 top priorities for today

1	☐
2	☐
3	☐

To do list	Water	Appointments

To do list		Water	Appointments
	☐		
	☐	1 ☐	
	☐	2 ☐	
	☐	3 ☐	
Schedule AM		4 ☐	**Schedule PM**
		5 ☐	
		6 ☐	
		7 ☐	
		8 ☐	

Food

B	D
L	S

Health & Fitness	I am thankful for...

Date:	Let's do this!	M T W T F S S

My 3 top priorities for today

1 ☐

2 ☐

3 ☐

To do list	Water	Appointments

To do list		Water	Appointments
☐		1	
☐		2 ☐	
☐		3 ☐	
☐		4 ☐	

Schedule AM		5 ☐	Schedule PM
		6 ☐	
		7 ☐	
		8 ☐	
		☐	

Food

B	D
L	S

Health & Fitness	I am thankful for...

Date: **Let's do this!**   M T W T F S S

My 3 top priorities for today

1   ☐

2   ☐

3   ☐

To do list	Water	Appointments
☐	1 ☐	
☐	2 ☐	
☐	3 ☐	
☐	4 ☐	
Schedule AM	5 ☐	**Schedule PM**
	6 ☐	
	7 ☐	
	8 ☐	
	☐	

Food

B	D
L	S

Health & Fitness	I am thankful for...

Date: _____ **Let's do this!** M T W T F S S

My 3 top priorities for today

1. ☐
2. ☐
3. ☐

To do list	Water	Appointments

☐
☐
☐
☐

Schedule AM

Schedule PM

Water:
1 ☐
2 ☐
3 ☐
4 ☐
5 ☐
6 ☐
7 ☐
8 ☐

Food

B

D

L

S

Health & Fitness	I am thankful for...

Date: Let's do this!   M T W T F S S

My 3 top priorities for today

1   ☐

2   ☐

3   ☐

To do list	Water	Appointments
☐	1 ☐	
☐	2 ☐	
☐	3 ☐	
☐	4 ☐	

Schedule AM   5 ☐   Schedule PM
                   6 ☐

                   7 ☐

                   8 ☐

Food

B   D

L   S

Health & Fitness   I am thankful for...

Date: **Let's do this!** M T W T F S S

My 3 top priorities for today

1 ☐

2 ☐

3 ☐

To do list	Water	Appointments

To do list:
- ☐
- ☐
- ☐
- ☐

Water:
1 ☐
2 ☐
3 ☐
4 ☐
5 ☐
6 ☐
7 ☐
8 ☐

Schedule AM

Schedule PM

Food

B

D

L

S

Health & Fitness	I am thankful for...

Date: _____ **Let's do this!** M T W T F S S

My 3 top priorities for today

1 _____ ☐

2 _____ ☐

3 _____ ☐

To do list	Water	Appointments

To do list		Water	Appointments
☐	1 ☐	
☐	2 ☐	
☐	3 ☐	
☐	4 ☐	

Schedule AM		Water	Schedule PM
	5 ☐	
	6 ☐	
	7 ☐	
	8 ☐	

Food

B	D
L	S

Health & Fitness	I am thankful for...

Date: _____   *Let's do this!*   M T W T F S S

My 3 top priorities for today

1 ☐

2 ☐

3 ☐

To do list	Water	Appointments

☐

☐

☐

☐

1 ☐
2 ☐
3 ☐
4 ☐
5 ☐
6 ☐
7 ☐
8 ☐

Schedule AM		Schedule PM

Food

B

D

L

S

Health & Fitness	I am thankful for...

Date: *Let's do this!*   M T W T F S S

My 3 top priorities for today

1   ☐

2   ☐

3   ☐

To do list	Water	Appointments
☐	1	
☐	2 ☐	
☐	3 ☐	
☐	4 ☐	

Schedule AM		Schedule PM
	5 ☐	
	6 ☐	
	7 ☐	
	8 ☐	

Food

B	D
L	S

Health & Fitness	I am thankful for...

Date: | **Let's do this!** | M T W T F S S

My 3 top priorities for today

1 ☐

2 ☐

3 ☐

To do list	Water	Appointments
☐	1 ☐	
☐	2 ☐	
☐	3 ☐	
☐	4 ☐	

Schedule AM		Schedule PM
	5 ☐	
	6 ☐	
	7 ☐	
	8 ☐	

Food

B	D
L	S

Health & Fitness	I am thankful for...

Date: _____   # Let's do this!   M T W T F S S

My 3 top priorities for today

1 _____ ☐

2 _____ ☐

3 _____ ☐

To do list	Water	Appointments

To do list		Water	Appointments
☐	1	
☐	2 ☐	
☐	3 ☐	
☐	4 ☐	

Schedule AM		Schedule PM
	5 ☐	
	6 ☐	
	7 ☐	
	8 ☐	

Food

B	D
L	S

Health & Fitness	I am thankful for...

Date: _____ **Let's do this!**   M T W T F S S

My 3 top priorities for today

1	☐
2	☐
3	☐

To do list	Water	Appointments

To do list			
	☐	1 ☐	
	☐	2 ☐	
	☐	3 ☐	
	☐	4 ☐	

Schedule AM		Schedule PM
	5 ☐	
	6 ☐	
	7 ☐	
	8 ☐	
	☐	

Food

B	D
L	S

Health & Fitness	I am thankful for...

Date: _____ Let's do this! M T W T F S S

My 3 top priorities for today

1 _____ ☐

2 _____ ☐

3 _____ ☐

To do list	Water	Appointments

To do list:
- ☐
- ☐
- ☐
- ☐

Water: 1 ☐ 2 ☐ 3 ☐ 4 ☐ 5 ☐ 6 ☐ 7 ☐ 8 ☐

Schedule AM

Schedule PM

Food

B	D
L	S

Health & Fitness	I am thankful for...

Date: _____ **Let's do this!** M T W T F S S

My 3 top priorities for today

1 _____ ☐

2 _____ ☐

3 _____ ☐

To do list	Water	Appointments

To do list ☐
☐ 1
☐ 2
☐ 3
☐ 4

Schedule AM	5	Schedule PM

6

7

8

Food

B | D

L | S

Health & Fitness	I am thankful for...

Date: | # Let's do this! | M T W T F S S

My 3 top priorities for today

1 ☐

2 ☐

3 ☐

To do list	Water	Appointments

☐
☐
☐
☐

1
☐ 2
☐ 3
☐ 4
☐ 5
☐ 6
☐ 7
☐ 8
☐

Schedule AM

Schedule PM

Food

B | D

L | S

Health & Fitness	I am thankful for...

Date: _____   Let's do this!   M T W T F S S

My 3 top priorities for today

1 _____ ☐

2 _____ ☐

3 _____ ☐

To do list	Water	Appointments

To do list:
- ☐
- ☐
- ☐
- ☐

Water:
1 ☐
2 ☐
3 ☐
4 ☐
5 ☐
6 ☐
7 ☐
8 ☐

Schedule AM

Schedule PM

Food

B _____

D _____

L _____

S _____

Health & Fitness	I am thankful for...

Date: | Let's do this! | M T W T F S S

My 3 top priorities for today

1 ☐

2 ☐

3 ☐

To do list	Water	Appointments
☐	1	
☐	☐ 2	
☐	☐ 3	
☐	☐ 4	

Schedule AM	☐ 5	Schedule PM
	☐ 6	
	☐ 7	
	☐ 8	
	☐	

Food

B	D
L	S

Health & Fitness	I am thankful for...

Date: _____   *Let's do this!*   M T W T F S S

My 3 top priorities for today

1 _____ ☐

2 _____ ☐

3 _____ ☐

To do list	Water	Appointments

To do list:
- ☐ _____
- ☐ _____
- ☐ _____
- ☐ _____

Schedule AM

Water:
1 ☐
2 ☐
3 ☐
4 ☐
5 ☐
6 ☐
7 ☐
8 ☐

Schedule PM

Food

B: _____   D: _____

L: _____   S: _____

Health & Fitness	I am thankful for...

Date:	Let's do this!	M T W T F S S

My 3 top priorities for today

1. ☐
2. ☐
3. ☐

To do list	Water	Appointments

To do list		Water	Appointments
	☐	1	
	☐	2 ☐	
	☐	3 ☐	
	☐	4 ☐	

Schedule AM	5 ☐	Schedule PM
	6 ☐	
	7 ☐	
	8 ☐	
	☐	

Food

B	D
L	S

Health & Fitness	I am thankful for...

Date: _____   Let's do this!   M T W T F S S

My 3 top priorities for today

1 _____ ☐

2 _____ ☐

3 _____ ☐

To do list	Water	Appointments

☐

☐

☐

☐

1 ☐
2 ☐
3 ☐
4 ☐
5 ☐
6 ☐
7 ☐
8 ☐

Schedule AM   Schedule PM

Food

B | D

L | S

Health & Fitness   I am thankful for...

Date: *Let's do this!*   M T W T F S S

My 3 top priorities for today

1   ☐

2   ☐

3   ☐

To do list	Water	Appointments
☐	1 ☐	
☐	2 ☐	
☐	3 ☐	
☐	4 ☐	

Schedule AM		Schedule PM
	5 ☐	
	6 ☐	
	7 ☐	
	8 ☐	

Food

B	D
L	S

Health & Fitness	I am thankful for...

Date:	Let's do this!	M T W T F S S

My 3 top priorities for today

1 ☐

2 ☐

3 ☐

To do list	Water	Appointments

☐

☐

☐

☐

1 ☐
2 ☐
3 ☐
4 ☐

Schedule AM

5 ☐

6 ☐

7 ☐

8 ☐

Schedule PM

Food

B

D

L

S

Health & Fitness	I am thankful for...

Date: _____ **Let's do this!**   M T W T F S S

My 3 top priorities for today

1 _____ ☐

2 _____ ☐

3 _____ ☐

To do list	Water	Appointments

☐

☐

☐

☐

1 ☐
2 ☐
3 ☐
4 ☐
5 ☐
6 ☐
7 ☐
8 ☐

Schedule AM   Schedule PM

Food

B | D

L | S

Health & Fitness   I am thankful for...

Date: _____ Let's do this!   M T W T F S S

My 3 top priorities for today

1 _____ ☐

2 _____ ☐

3 _____ ☐

To do list	Water	Appointments

To do list ☐

☐

☐

☐

Water
1 ☐
2 ☐
3 ☐
4 ☐
5 ☐
6 ☐
7 ☐
8 ☐

Schedule AM

Schedule PM

Food

B _____ | D _____

L _____ | S _____

Health & Fitness | I am thankful for...

Date: **Let's do this!**   M T W T F S S

My 3 top priorities for today

1 ☐

2 ☐

3 ☐

To do list	Water	Appointments
☐	1 ☐	
☐	2 ☐	
☐	3 ☐	
☐	4 ☐	

Schedule AM		Schedule PM
	5 ☐	
	6 ☐	
	7 ☐	
	8 ☐	

Food

B	D
L	S

Health & Fitness	I am thankful for...

Date:	Let's do this!	M T W T F S S

My 3 top priorities for today

1 ☐

2 ☐

3 ☐

To do list	Water	Appointments

☐

☐

☐

☐

1 ☐
2 ☐
3 ☐
4 ☐
5 ☐
6 ☐
7 ☐
8 ☐

Schedule AM

Schedule PM

Food

B

D

L

S

Health & Fitness	I am thankful for...

Date: _____ **Let's do this!** M T W T F S S

My 3 top priorities for today

1 _____ ☐

2 _____ ☐

3 _____ ☐

To do list	Water	Appointments

To do list:
- ☐
- ☐
- ☐
- ☐

Water:
1 ☐
2 ☐
3 ☐
4 ☐
5 ☐
6 ☐
7 ☐
8 ☐

Schedule AM

Schedule PM

Food

B _____ D _____

L _____ S _____

Health & Fitness	I am thankful for...

Date: _____ Let's do this! M T W T F S S

My 3 top priorities for today

1 ☐

2 ☐

3 ☐

To do list	Water	Appointments

☐

☐

☐

☐

1
☐
2
☐
3
☐
4
☐
5
☐
6
☐
7
☐
8
☐

Schedule AM		Schedule PM

Food

B | D

L | S

Health & Fitness	I am thankful for...

Date: Let's do this!   M T W T F S S

My 3 top priorities for today

1 ☐

2 ☐

3 ☐

To do list	Water	Appointments

To do list:
- ☐
- ☐
- ☐
- ☐

Water:
1 ☐
2 ☐
3 ☐
4 ☐
5 ☐
6 ☐
7 ☐
8 ☐

Schedule AM

Schedule PM

Food

B

D

L

S

Health & Fitness	I am thankful for...

Date: _____ Let's do this!   M T W T F S S

My 3 top priorities for today

1	☐
2	☐
3	☐

To do list	Water	Appointments

To do list		Water	Appointments
	☐		
		1 ☐	
	☐	2 ☐	
	☐	3 ☐	
	☐	4 ☐	

Schedule AM		Schedule PM
	5 ☐	
	6 ☐	
	7 ☐	
	8 ☐	

Food

B	D
L	S

Health & Fitness	I am thankful for...

Date: *Let's do this!*   M T W T F S S

My 3 top priorities for today

1   ☐

2   ☐

3   ☐

To do list	Water	Appointments
☐	1 ☐	
☐	2 ☐	
☐	3 ☐	
☐	4 ☐	

Schedule AM	Water	Schedule PM
	5 ☐	
	6 ☐	
	7 ☐	
	8 ☐	

Food

B	D
L	S

Health & Fitness	I am thankful for...

Date: _____   *Let's do this!*   M T W T F S S

My 3 top priorities for today

1 _____ ☐

2 _____ ☐

3 _____ ☐

To do list	Water	Appointments

To do list		Water	Appointments
☐	1 ☐	
☐	2 ☐	
☐	3 ☐	
☐	4 ☐	

Schedule AM		Schedule PM
	5 ☐	
	6 ☐	
	7 ☐	
	8 ☐	
	☐	

Food

B	D
L	S

Health & Fitness	I am thankful for...

Date: _____ **Let's do this!**   M T W T F S S

My 3 top priorities for today

1	☐
2	☐
3	☐

To do list	Water	Appointments

☐	1 ☐	
☐	2 ☐	
☐	3 ☐	
☐	4 ☐	

Schedule AM		Schedule PM
	5 ☐	
	6 ☐	
	7 ☐	
	8 ☐	

Food

B	D
L	S

Health & Fitness	I am thankful for...

Date: _____ Let's do this!   M T W T F S S

My 3 top priorities for today

1 _____ ☐

2 _____ ☐

3 _____ ☐

To do list	Water	Appointments

☐	1	
☐	☐ 2	
☐	☐ 3	
☐	☐ 4	

Schedule AM	☐ 5	Schedule PM
	☐ 6	
	☐ 7	
	☐ 8	
	☐	

Food

B	D
L	S

Health & Fitness	I am thankful for...

Date:	Let's do this!	M T W T F S S

My 3 top priorities for today

1	☐
2	☐
3	☐

To do list	Water	Appointments

To do list		Water	Appointments
	☐	1 ☐	
	☐	2 ☐	
	☐	3 ☐	
	☐	4 ☐	

Schedule AM	Water	Schedule PM
	5 ☐	
	6 ☐	
	7 ☐	
	8 ☐	

Food

B	D
L	S

Health & Fitness	I am thankful for...

Date: Let's do this!   M T W T F S S

My 3 top priorities for today

1   ☐

2   ☐

3   ☐

To do list	Water	Appointments
☐	1 ☐	
☐	2 ☐	
☐	3 ☐	
☐	4 ☐	

Schedule AM	5 ☐	Schedule PM
	6 ☐	
	7 ☐	
	8 ☐	
	☐	

Food

B	D
L	S

Health & Fitness	I am thankful for...

Date: _____ *Let's do this!* M T W T F S S

My 3 top priorities for today

1 ☐

2 ☐

3 ☐

To do list	Water	Appointments

To do list		Water	Appointments
☐	1 ☐	
☐	2 ☐	
☐	3 ☐	
☐	4 ☐	

Schedule AM		Schedule PM
	5 ☐	
	6 ☐	
	7 ☐	
	8 ☐	

Food

B	D
L	S

Health & Fitness	I am thankful for...

Date: _____ *Let's do this!* M T W T F S S

My 3 top priorities for today

1. ☐
2. ☐
3. ☐

To do list	Water	Appointments
☐		
☐	1 ☐	
☐	2 ☐	
☐	3 ☐	

Schedule AM		Schedule PM
	4 ☐	
	5 ☐	
	6 ☐	
	7 ☐	
	8 ☐	

Food

B	D
L	S

Health & Fitness	I am thankful for...

Date:	Let's do this!	M T W T F S S

My 3 top priorities for today

1. ☐
2. ☐
3. ☐

To do list	Water	Appointments

To do list		Water	Appointments
	☐	1 ☐	
	☐	2 ☐	
	☐	3 ☐	
	☐	4 ☐	
Schedule AM		5 ☐	Schedule PM
		6 ☐	
		7 ☐	
		8 ☐	

Food

B	D
L	S

Health & Fitness	I am thankful for...

Date: # Let's do this!   M T W T F S S

My 3 top priorities for today

1   ☐

2   ☐

3   ☐

To do list	Water	Appointments
☐	1 ☐	
☐	2 ☐	
☐	3 ☐	
☐	4 ☐	

Schedule AM	Water	Schedule PM
	5 ☐	
	6 ☐	
	7 ☐	
	8 ☐	

Food

B	D
L	S

Health & Fitness	I am thankful for...

Date: _____   Let's do this!   M T W T F S S

My 3 top priorities for today

1 _____ ☐

2 _____ ☐

3 _____ ☐

To do list	Water	Appointments

To do list		Water	Appointments
☐	1 ☐	
☐	2 ☐	
☐	3 ☐	
☐	4 ☐	

Schedule AM			Schedule PM
	5 ☐		
	6 ☐		
	7 ☐		
	8 ☐		

Food

B	D
L	S

Health & Fitness	I am thankful for...

Date: _____ **Let's do this!** M T W T F S S

My 3 top priorities for today

1 ☐

2 ☐

3 ☐

To do list	Water	Appointments

To do list:
- ☐
- ☐
- ☐
- ☐

Water:
1 ☐
2 ☐
3 ☐
4 ☐
5 ☐
6 ☐
7 ☐
8 ☐

Schedule AM

Schedule PM

Food

B

D

L

S

Health & Fitness

I am thankful for...

Date: _____ **Let's do this!** M T W T F S S

My 3 top priorities for today

1 _____ ☐

2 _____ ☐

3 _____ ☐

To do list	Water	Appointments

☐

☐

☐

☐

1 ☐
2 ☐
3 ☐
4 ☐
5 ☐
6 ☐
7 ☐
8 ☐

Schedule AM

Schedule PM

Food

B _____ D _____

L _____ S _____

Health & Fitness	I am thankful for...

Date: _____ **Let's do this!** M T W T F S S

My 3 top priorities for today

1	☐
2	☐
3	☐

To do list	Water	Appointments

To do list		Water	Appointments
	☐	1 ☐	
	☐	2 ☐	
	☐	3 ☐	
	☐	4 ☐	

Schedule AM / Schedule PM

Schedule AM	Water	Schedule PM
	5 ☐	
	6 ☐	
	7 ☐	
	8 ☐	
	☐	

Food

B	D
L	S

Health & Fitness	I am thankful for...

Date: _____ Let's do this! M T W T F S S

My 3 top priorities for today

1. ☐
2. ☐
3. ☐

To do list	Water	Appointments
☐	1 ☐	
☐	2 ☐	
☐	3 ☐	
☐	4 ☐	

Schedule AM	Water	Schedule PM
	5 ☐	
	6 ☐	
	7 ☐	
	8 ☐	

Food

B	D
L	S

Health & Fitness	I am thankful for...

Date: _____ *Let's do this!* M T W T F S S

My 3 top priorities for today

1 _____ ☐

2 _____ ☐

3 _____ ☐

To do list	Water	Appointments

☐

☐

☐

☐

Water:
1 ☐
2 ☐
3 ☐
4 ☐
5 ☐
6 ☐
7 ☐
8 ☐

Schedule AM		Schedule PM

Food

B _____ | D _____

L _____ | S _____

Health & Fitness	I am thankful for...

Date: **Let's do this!** M T W T F S S

My 3 top priorities for today

1 ☐

2 ☐

3 ☐

To do list	Water	Appointments

☐

☐

☐

☐

Schedule AM		Schedule PM

1 ☐
2 ☐
3 ☐
4 ☐
5 ☐
6 ☐
7 ☐
8 ☐

Food

B | D

L | S

Health & Fitness	I am thankful for...

Date:	Let's do this!	M T W T F S S

My 3 top priorities for today

1 ☐

2 ☐

3 ☐

To do list	Water	Appointments

To do list:
- ☐
- ☐
- ☐
- ☐

Water:
1 ☐
2 ☐
3 ☐
4 ☐
5 ☐
6 ☐
7 ☐
8 ☐

Schedule AM

Schedule PM

Food

B

D

L

S

Health & Fitness

I am thankful for...

Date: _____   **Let's do this!**   M T W T F S S

My 3 top priorities for today

1 ☐

2 ☐

3 ☐

To do list	Water	Appointments

To do list:
- ☐
- ☐
- ☐
- ☐

Schedule AM

Water:
1 ☐
2 ☐
3 ☐
4 ☐
5 ☐
6 ☐
7 ☐
8 ☐

Schedule PM

Food

B

D

L

S

Health & Fitness	I am thankful for...

Date:	Let's do this!	M T W T F S S

My 3 top priorities for today

1 ☐

2 ☐

3 ☐

To do list	Water	Appointments

To do list		Water	Appointments
☐	1 ☐	
☐	2 ☐	
☐	3 ☐	
☐	4 ☐	

Schedule AM		Water	Schedule PM
	5 ☐	
	6 ☐	
	7 ☐	
	8 ☐	

Food

B	D
L	S

Health & Fitness	I am thankful for...

Date: # Let's do this!   M T W T F S S

My 3 top priorities for today

1   ☐

2   ☐

3   ☐

To do list	Water	Appointments
☐	1 ☐	
☐	2 ☐	
☐	3 ☐	
☐	4 ☐	

Schedule AM		Schedule PM
	5 ☐	
	6 ☐	
	7 ☐	
	8 ☐	

Food

B	D
L	S

Health & Fitness	I am thankful for...

Date: _____   **Let's do this!**   M T W T F S S

My 3 top priorities for today

1	☐
2	☐
3	☐

To do list	Water	Appointments

To do list	Water	Appointments
☐	1 ☐	
☐	2 ☐	
☐	3 ☐	
☐	4 ☐	

Schedule AM		Schedule PM
	5 ☐	
	6 ☐	
	7 ☐	
	8 ☐	

Food

B	D
L	S

Health & Fitness	I am thankful for...

Date: _____ **Let's do this!** M T W T F S S

My 3 top priorities for today

1 _____ ☐

2 _____ ☐

3 _____ ☐

To do list	Water	Appointments

☐ _____

☐ _____

☐ _____

☐ _____

1 ☐
2 ☐
3 ☐
4 ☐
5 ☐
6 ☐
7 ☐
8 ☐

Schedule AM

Schedule PM

Food

B _____ D _____

L _____ S _____

Health & Fitness	I am thankful for...

Date:	Let's do this!	M T W T F S S

My 3 top priorities for today

1 ☐

2 ☐

3 ☐

To do list	Water	Appointments
☐	1 ☐	
☐	2 ☐	
☐	3 ☐	
☐	4 ☐	

Schedule AM	5 ☐	Schedule PM
	6 ☐	
	7 ☐	
	8 ☐	
	☐	

Food

B	D
L	S

Health & Fitness	I am thankful for...

Date: _____   # Let's do this!   M T W T F S S

My 3 top priorities for today

1 _____ ☐

2 _____ ☐

3 _____ ☐

To do list	Water	Appointments

To do list
- ☐
- ☐
- ☐
- ☐

Water
1 ☐
2 ☐
3 ☐
4 ☐
5 ☐
6 ☐
7 ☐
8 ☐

Schedule AM

Schedule PM

Food

B	D
L	S

Health & Fitness	I am thankful for...

Date: Let's do this!   M T W T F S S

My 3 top priorities for today

1 ☐

2 ☐

3 ☐

To do list	Water	Appointments

☐

☐   1 ☐

☐   2 ☐

☐   3 ☐

Schedule AM	4 ☐	Schedule PM

5 ☐

6 ☐

7 ☐

8 ☐

Food

B   D

L   S

Health & Fitness	I am thankful for...

Date: _____ *Let's do this!* M T W T F S S

My 3 top priorities for today

1. ☐
2. ☐
3. ☐

To do list	Water	Appointments
☐	1 ☐	
☐	2 ☐	
☐	3 ☐	
☐	4 ☐	

Schedule AM	5 ☐	Schedule PM
	6 ☐	
	7 ☐	
	8 ☐	
	☐	

Food

B	D
L	S

Health & Fitness	I am thankful for...

Date: _____ **Let's do this!** M T W T F S S

My 3 top priorities for today

1 _____ ☐

2 _____ ☐

3 _____ ☐

To do list	Water	Appointments
☐	1	
☐	☐ 2	
☐	☐ 3	
☐	☐ 4	

Schedule AM		Schedule PM
	☐ 5	
	☐ 6	
	☐ 7	
	☐ 8	
	☐	

Food

B	D
L	S

Health & Fitness	I am thankful for...

Date: _____ Let's do this! M T W T F S S

My 3 top priorities for today

1 _____ ☐

2 _____ ☐

3 _____ ☐

To do list	Water	Appointments

☐

☐

☐

☐

1
☐
2
☐
3
☐
4
☐
5
☐
6
☐
7
☐
8
☐

Schedule AM

Schedule PM

Food

B | D

L | S

Health & Fitness | I am thankful for...

Date: Let's do this!   M T W T F S S

My 3 top priorities for today

1 ☐

2 ☐

3 ☐

To do list	Water	Appointments

To do list:
- ☐
- ☐
- ☐
- ☐

Schedule AM

Water:
1 ☐
2 ☐
3 ☐
4 ☐
5 ☐
6 ☐
7 ☐
8 ☐

Schedule PM

Food

B

D

L

S

Health & Fitness	I am thankful for...

Date: Let's do this!   M T W T F S S

My 3 top priorities for today

1   ☐

2   ☐

3   ☐

To do list	Water	Appointments
☐	1	
☐	☐ 2	
☐	☐ 3	
☐	☐ 4	

Schedule AM		Schedule PM
	☐ 5	
	☐ 6	
	☐ 7	
	☐ 8	
	☐	

Food

B	D
L	S

Health & Fitness	I am thankful for...

Date: *Let's do this!*   M T W T F S S

My 3 top priorities for today

1 ☐

2 ☐

3 ☐

To do list	Water	Appointments

☐

☐

☐

☐

1
☐
2
☐
3
☐
4
☐
5
☐
6
☐
7
☐
8
☐

Schedule AM		Schedule PM

Food

B

D

L

S

Health & Fitness	I am thankful for...

Date:	Let's do this!	M T W T F S S

My 3 top priorities for today

1   ☐

2   ☐

3   ☐

To do list	Water	Appointments
☐	1 ☐	
☐	2 ☐	
☐	3 ☐	
☐	4 ☐	

Schedule AM	5 ☐	Schedule PM
	6 ☐	
	7 ☐	
	8 ☐	

Food

B	D
L	S

Health & Fitness	I am thankful for...

Date: *Let's do this!*   M T W T F S S

My 3 top priorities for today

1   ☐

2   ☐

3   ☐

To do list	Water	Appointments
☐	1 ☐	
☐	2 ☐	
☐	3 ☐	
☐	4 ☐	

Schedule AM		Schedule PM
	5 ☐	
	6 ☐	
	7 ☐	
	8 ☐	

Food

B

D

L

S

Health & Fitness	I am thankful for...

Date: *Let's do this!*   M T W T F S S

My 3 top priorities for today

1   ☐

2   ☐

3   ☐

To do list	Water	Appointments

To do list:
- ☐
- ☐
- ☐
- ☐

Water:
1 ☐
2 ☐
3 ☐
4 ☐
5 ☐
6 ☐
7 ☐
8 ☐

Schedule AM		Schedule PM

Food

B	D
L	S

Health & Fitness	I am thankful for...

Date:	Let's do this!	M T W T F S S

My 3 top priorities for today

1. ☐
2. ☐
3. ☐

To do list	Water	Appointments
☐	1	
☐	☐ 2	
☐	☐ 3	
☐	☐ 4	

Schedule AM	☐ 5	Schedule PM
	☐ 6	
	☐ 7	
	☐ 8	
	☐	

Food

B	D
L	S

Health & Fitness	I am thankful for...

Date: _____   # Let's do this!   M T W T F S S

My 3 top priorities for today

1. ☐

2. ☐

3. ☐

To do list	Water	Appointments

To do list
- ☐
- ☐
- ☐
- ☐

Water
1 ☐
2 ☐
3 ☐
4 ☐
5 ☐
6 ☐
7 ☐
8 ☐

Schedule AM

Schedule PM

Food

B

D

L

S

Health & Fitness

I am thankful for...

Date: _____   *Let's do this!*   M T W T F S S

My 3 top priorities for today

1 _____ ☐

2 _____ ☐

3 _____ ☐

To do list	Water	Appointments

To do list
- ☐ _____
- ☐ _____
- ☐ _____
- ☐ _____

Schedule AM

Water
1 ☐
2 ☐
3 ☐
4 ☐
5 ☐
6 ☐
7 ☐
8 ☐

Schedule PM

Food

B _____   D _____

L _____   S _____

Health & Fitness	I am thankful for...

Date: _____   *Let's do this!*   M T W T F S S

My 3 top priorities for today

1 _____ ☐

2 _____ ☐

3 _____ ☐

To do list	Water	Appointments

To do list		Water	Appointments
	☐	1 ☐	
	☐	2 ☐	
	☐	3 ☐	
	☐	4 ☐	

Schedule AM		Schedule PM
	5 ☐	
	6 ☐	
	7 ☐	
	8 ☐	

Food

B	D
L	S

Health & Fitness	I am thankful for...

Date: **Let's do this!**   M T W T F S S

My 3 top priorities for today

1   ☐

2   ☐

3   ☐

To do list	Water	Appointments
☐	1 ☐	
☐	2 ☐	
☐	3 ☐	
☐	4 ☐	

Schedule AM		Schedule PM
	5 ☐	
	6 ☐	
	7 ☐	
	8 ☐	

Food

B

D

L

S

Health & Fitness	I am thankful for...

Date: _____ # Let's do this! M T W T F S S

My 3 top priorities for today

1 _____ ☐

2 _____ ☐

3 _____ ☐

To do list	Water	Appointments

	☐			
	☐	1 ☐		
	☐	2 ☐		
	☐	3 ☐		

Schedule AM

4 ☐

5 ☐

6 ☐

7 ☐

8 ☐

Schedule PM

Food

B	D
L	S

Health & Fitness	I am thankful for...

| Date: | Let's do this! | M T W T F S S |

My 3 top priorities for today

1 ☐

2 ☐

3 ☐

| To do list | Water | Appointments |

☐

☐

☐

☐

1 ☐
2 ☐
3 ☐
4 ☐
5 ☐
6 ☐
7 ☐
8 ☐

Schedule AM

Schedule PM

Food

B

D

L

S

Health & Fitness

I am thankful for...

Date: # Let's do this!   M T W T F S S

My 3 top priorities for today

1   ☐

2   ☐

3   ☐

To do list	Water	Appointments
☐	1	
☐	☐ 2	
☐	☐ 3	
☐	☐ 4	

Schedule AM

	Water	Schedule PM
	☐ 5	
	☐ 6	
	☐ 7	
	☐ 8	
	☐	

Food

B	D
L	S

Health & Fitness	I am thankful for...

Date: Let's do this!   M T W T F S S

My 3 top priorities for today

1   ☐

2   ☐

3   ☐

To do list	Water	Appointments
☐	1 ☐	
☐	2 ☐	
☐	3 ☐	
☐	4 ☐	

Schedule AM		Schedule PM
	5 ☐	
	6 ☐	
	7 ☐	
	8 ☐	

Food

B	D
L	S

Health & Fitness	I am thankful for...

Date:	*Let's do this!*	M T W T F S S

My 3 top priorities for today

1 ☐

2 ☐

3 ☐

To do list	Water	Appointments

☐
☐
☐
☐

1 ☐
2 ☐
3 ☐
4 ☐
5 ☐
6 ☐
7 ☐
8 ☐

Schedule AM

Schedule PM

Food

B	D
L	S

Health & Fitness	I am thankful for...

Date: _____   **Let's do this!**   M T W T F S S

My 3 top priorities for today

1 _____ ☐

2 _____ ☐

3 _____ ☐

To do list	Water	Appointments

To do list		Water	Appointments
☐	1 ☐	
☐	2 ☐	
☐	3 ☐	
☐	4 ☐	

Schedule AM		Schedule PM
	5 ☐	
	6 ☐	
	7 ☐	
	8 ☐	

Food

B	D
L	S

Health & Fitness	I am thankful for...

Made in United States
North Haven, CT
07 November 2022

26388009R00070